Your A

W

15 Key Steps to Manifesting True Health and Lasting Wellness

Did you know your words have meaning? Do you feel like your life isn't going anywhere and you keep repeating the same things over and over again? Have you ever felt powerless and unable to move forward? These are questions we all face at one time or another, and there are solutions to them. In this Itty Bitty® book, Dr. Dolores Fazzino will guide you to experience your life in a positive and powerful way. You will learn to make peace with uncertainty and fear through listening and trusting your inner wisdom. You will come away with the tools to show up in your life; aligning your mind, body and soul.

In addition, you will learn:

- Self-respect
- Emotional confidence
- Personal empowerment
- And so much more

If you are ready to take control of your life in a loving appreciative way pick up a copy of this must-read Itty Bitty® book today!

Your Amazing Itty Bitty® Healing in Ways You Never Thought Possible Book

15 Key Steps To Manifesting True Health and Lasting Wellness

Dr. Dolores Fazzino, DNP

Published by Itty Bitty® Publishing
A subsidiary of S & P Productions, Inc.

Printed in the United States of America

Itty Bitty Publishing
311 Main Street, Suite D
El Segundo, CA 90245
(310) 640-8885

ISBN: 978-1-950326-85-3

Dedication Page

I dedicate this book to all those who have been part of my life for a reason, a season, and/or a lifetime. You have given me some of my most profound growth opportunities, allowing me to go deeper, to have a better relationship with myself and to remember who I am at a soul level.

I am forever grateful for the wisdom I have gained with every experience, from the most amazing to the most challenging ones on my life's journey. These growth opportunities have made me the unique person that I am today, which has enabled me to assist and inspire my clients to embrace their lives and enjoy the journey.

Stop by our Itty Bitty® website to find more interesting information regarding …

www.IttyBittyPublishing.com

Or visit Dr. Dolores Fazzino, DNP, RN, Nurse Practitioner, Medical Intuitive at:

www.DrDoloresFazzino.com

Table of Contents

Introduction

Feeling stuck, in a rut, and can't figure out how to get out of it?

Do you ever feel like your life is just like the movie *Groundhog Day?* You wake up each day and it's the same theme, but a different variation?

Or how about this: Do you ever feel as if you are driving through life with your emergency brake on? I know we've all felt that way!

Have you ever opened a bag of Purina Dog Chow? It's the one with the string, and if you pull it in the wrong direction, it bunches up and locks itself. Yet when you pull the string in the correct direction, the opening unravels, and the dog chow is ready to serve.

If you have ever experienced one or several of these situations, you know you're not alone. I too, have experienced them.

What I have learned from my life experiences is that everything starts with "me" first. YES, everything starts with yourself first. Creating the life of your dreams is an inside job.

What I teach is rarely taught to us at a young age, and if it were, imagine what your potential would be!

Rest assured that timing is everything. Now is the time to learn and implement the foundation of spiritual wellness for life and the fifteen keys to wellness.

These keys may or may not be the ones that you feel are important, yet they lay a solid foundation to build your life upon.

So, let's start your journey …

Step 1
Becoming Your Own Best Friend

The longest relationship you will ever have in your life is the one you have with yourself. Yet, we often treat ourselves rather poorly.

1. Do you nourish, respect, appreciate, and most importantly, love yourself properly?
2. You are in crisis. The noise of your external world can distract you from listening to your inner wisdom, where all your answers are.
3. More than ever there is noise, chaos and uncertainty in the world. This makes it challenging to discern the correct path to choose regarding any decision you need to make.
4. The problem is you are detached from your body and who you truly are. You are constantly in your head, misaligned, and even disconnected from your body.

Your body suffers the long-term consequences of these effects, possibly through disease or injury.

Easy Tips to Help You To Learn To Reconnect With Your Body

- Make yourself a priority in life. Give yourself permission to do so. If you don't do this for yourself, no one else will.
- Take a vacation from electronic devices. Turn off social media, news, your devices, and any other distractions.
- Spend time in nature. Go for walks or hike. Even if you live in a city, there are parks; spend some time there.
- Take deep breaths. Deep breathing brings more relaxation into your physical body.
- Spend time with your animal companions. Animals are about being in their bodies, being spontaneous and in the moment.
- Spend time with children. They, too, are spontaneous, in the moment, highly creative, and have great imaginations.
- Movement and activity are important. Take up yoga, Qi Gong, dancing, or walking for at least 15 minutes without electronic devices. Experience what you are feeling and journal about it.

Step 2
Your Words Have Meaning: Choose Them Wisely!

Did you know that everything is energy and has a frequency, including your emotions, thoughts, and beliefs? This is true!

1. Even your self-talk is energy that affects your entire body, mind, and soul. Avoid critical self-talk that acts as punishment for being less than perfect.
2. Dr. Masuro Emoto, who studied water consciousness, showed that when containers of water were labeled with high-frequency words such as *love, peace, healing,* crystal formations upon freezing, generated beautiful symmetrical crystals. But when water was labeled with low-vibrating words like *hate, kill, ugly,* the crystal formations from the water were fragmented, unformed, and asymmetrical.
3. Your body is 70% water; keep its water composition positive!

Tame and Shift Your Self-Talk

In general, you tend to treat others better than you treat yourself, and you hold yourself to a higher standard. Following are tips to improve your self-talk.

- Become aware. Once you know your self-talk is negative, you have a choice to change it.
- Notice what triggers your counter-productive self-talk. Sometimes you're just on automatic pilot and react instead of being aware and responsive.
- Be a work in progress.
- Take baby steps. This pattern within you was not created overnight and may take time to shift.
- If you fall off the wagon, catch yourself and create something more positive.
- Would you say the things you say to yourself to your best friend? Treat yourself as if you were speaking to that special friend.

Step 3
Giving Your Power Away

As a healthcare provider for over 40 years, I have seen people give their power of decision making regarding their health and wellness to something outside of themselves, in this case, the healthcare system.

1. In truth, you have access to your own inner physician, the innate wisdom you carry in your body. Unfortunately, you rarely tap into this advice and by default take the advice of something outside of you to help make decisions.
2. Though subtle, this is an example of giving your power away to something outside of yourself.
3. Have you ever felt that you shouldn't do something, but you ignore it and do it anyway, then live to regret your decision? This is an example of not listening to your inner wisdom and giving your power away to something outside of yourself.

Take Back Your Power and Your Life

Once you are aware of what is happening, you have a choice as to what you want to create for yourself.

Some things to reflect upon:

- Where in your life do you give your power away? With your health, your relationships, or something else?
- Ever have those inner wisdom moments where you decided not to trust that knowledge, chose something different, and lived to regret it?
- Connect to your inner wisdom, that voice within which allows you to access your body, mind, and soul needs.

Some things to try out:

- **Listen for your inner wisdom and trust it**. The first thing you feel, hear, or sense is usually the right response. We often talk ourselves out of it, rationalize, or justify ourselves.
- **Quiet your mind.** Listen to relaxing instrumental music, music of high hertz frequency, or a guided meditation to ground yourself into your body.

Step 4
Healthy Boundaries

There are two types of boundaries: the physical, the ones which are visible (such as a fence around a property) and the non-physical (such as the mental and emotional) which are invisible and intangible. Both are addressed here.

1. Nonphysical boundaries such as emotions, thoughts, or beliefs are fluid. They wax and wane with an ebb and flow aspect to them.
2. Everything is energy whether it is visible or invisible. Sometimes the boundaries are difficult to discern, particularly if you are unaware of them.
3. Are you sensitive and tend to take on other people's feelings, emotions, and ideas? Do you feel you do not know where your energy ends and where someone else's begins? Do you feel exhausted when you are around certain people and do not know why?

Enmeshed Boundaries

To clarify, you may be unclear where you end and where another person begins. This creates confusion, chaos, and drama in your life because you are unconsciously taking on other people's issues and *stuff* as your own.

Some key points to remember:

- Once you realize this is happening, you can change the pattern. Being aware is the first step.
- Remove yourself from those situations, people, and things that drain you energetically and observe how you start to get your energy back.

The best way to create an energetic boundary is to set one. Reciting this statement below will help:

> "If this is not my energy, by the laws of the universe, it must leave immediately."

You have free will on this earth; nothing can interfere with it unless you allow it. Often, we allow things into our energy field consciously as well as unconsciously. Reciting the phrase above will shift your space, allowing you to have more freedom, discernment, and feel re-energized.

Step 5
It's OK To Feel Your Emotions: Your Emotions Are a Gift!

Emotions have gotten a bad rap. Society has taught us that having or expressing emotions is taboo and unacceptable, particularly the ones that are labeled as not so positive—anger, rage, unhappiness, disappointment.

1. All emotions are good, whether you label them good or bad. When you allow yourself to experience emotions, you are creating a healthier body and lasting wellness.
2. Emotions are energy. When you allow yourself to experience them, the energy is neutralized and dissipates. When you do not experience your emotions, possibly stuffing them, ignoring them, shelving them for a later time, or even partially experiencing them, the energy gets trapped in pockets.
3. Over time, these pockets continue to expand and grow, especially if you control your emotions and intellectualize them. Eventually, unexperienced emotions may create physical conditions and even cancer.

So, Feel Away!

It is very telling as to whether you are experienceing your emotions or intellectualizing them. Do you say, "I think, I feel?" If you do, then you are intellectualizing, hiding your feelings, and observing them from the stadium seats of your life.

Or are you afraid to experience them for fear of opening Pandora's Box of uncertainty, and being unable to close the box lid?

I invite you to try the following:

- Lean into your emotions, to feel them and experience them. Be with what you are experiencing. This too shall pass.
- Experience your emotions and don't project those feelings onto others.
- As you experience and feel your emotions, feel the release occurring in your body, mind and soul.
- Give yourself permission to be vulnerable. Surround yourself with others who listen, hold the space and do not allow others to fix it for you.

Step 6
Self-Respect

Self-respect is holding yourself in esteem and believing you are good and worthy of being treated well. It is like a boundary within a boundary.

1. It is setting limits as to what you will and will not tolerate. It is a foundational step to creating true health and lasting wellness.
2. Do you ever feel that you have to ask permission to do everything in your life? Or that you're staying in a job you know you should leave because you're not following your passion but your pay-check and benefits instead?
3. Are you in a relationship that is no longer satisfying or gratifying?
4. Are you staying in an abusive relationship because you're afraid of being alone and something is better than nothing, or are you relying on your relationship for your financial security?

Take a deep breath and congratulate yourself, because you may have realized for the first time in your life that you have choices and the ability to create something different!

Self-Respect a Little Deeper

How you treat yourself paves the way to how others treat you. Yes, another law of attraction thing, and it's very true!

When you look for your worth outside your-self, you may take on the projections of others as your truth and unconsciously try to fix them. To better understand yourself, I invite you to take a personal inventory. This is a list of situations where you may have given your personal power away either consciously or unconsciously, possibly because you did not know any better.

- List any situation where you were not respected, valued, honored, or appreciated for who you are.
- Have you been bullied, either physically, mentally, emotionally, and/or spiritually? List those as well.
- Ever feel not good enough, unworthy, or not loveable? List those as well.
- Remember, no one can disrespect you unless you allow them to.
- Love yourself enough to take charge and don't hesitate to call out others when they disrespect you!
- Respecting yourself is EXTREME SELF-CARE!

Step 7
Help! I'm Being Triggered: Self-Worth

By now, you realize that everything begins with you. If you see something that you don't like outside of you, there is an aspect of that very thing that triggers you or pushes the buttons inside of you.

1. Usually this happens unconsciously within you. You always have a choice: you can react to the situation or respond to the situation. You can be a victim (a choice) or do something about it (also, a choice).
2. Who you are is reflected back to you. This is called mirroring.
3. If you have poor self-worth and tend to give your personal power away to others and to situations outside yourself, you also may not have great respect for yourself and vice versa.
4. If you have weak self-respect or no self-respect, you may have low self-worth. Even though I believe there are shades of gray in most situations, I feel there is a strong correlation between the two.

Triggering, Self-Worth, and Personal Power: The Trifecta

You have most likely given your personal power away to others or to a situation, either consciously or unconsciously, at some point or time in your life. I know that I have.

- Use your personal power when you respond: You can react to triggers or be mindful of your responses.
- How you respond to triggering says a lot about your self-worth.
- Embrace controversy, share your voice. You are worth being supported, loved, appreciated and valued for yourself.
- Get over "what others will think," or not rocking the boat to "keep the peace" at your own personal expense and self-worth.
- Be mindful about giving away your personal power, your civil rights, your sovereignty to others, to institutions, and even to your government.
- Be authentic and genuine.
- Believe in yourself, put yourself first.
- Burn the door mat; you have every right to have all your needs met. You have to start believing this!

All of this may seem uncomfortable, yet it is a necessary aspect to gaining self-worth and being in your personal power!

Step 8
Self-Forgiveness

Forgiveness is a rather "touchy" subject for many; self-forgiveness is even more so. It is the cornerstone to true health and lasting wellness.

1. Your ego controls the situation and needs to be right no matter what the cost.
2. You are hardest on yourself.
3. When you do not forgive yourself, hold grudges, or partially forgive, you are only hurting yourself.
4. Forgiving but not forgetting is incomplete forgiveness. It's like a string that is still attached to the situation and is still incomplete.
5. Forgiveness liberates you. It creates the space for you to experience miracles in your life.

Three Aspects of Self-Forgiveness

Did you know that there are three important aspects to self-forgiveness?

- **Forgiving others**. Everything someone else has done to you, you have also done to them as well, whether you believe so or not.
- **Asking forgiveness of others.** Since you have done this very act to others as well, you must also ask forgiveness of others for the very act that was done to you by them.

Take a breath …

- **Most importantly, forgive yourself.** Since you tend to beat yourself up consciously or unconsciously, it is important to forgive yourself for the very act that was done to you by others, which *you* have done to others, and for that very act you have done to yourself as well.

You may also try:

- Reflecting on things that you are unaware of that are unresolved issues of forgiveness.
- Being kind to yourself. You are loved more than you know.

Step 9
Reflection

Life is fast-paced, and time seems to move faster and faster. It's easy to get caught up in the day-to-day flow without enough time in the day to do everything you'd like to accomplish. You may be stressed, anxious, and feel like you're constantly running a race to get through your day, or what's more, your life.

1. You find it hard to slow down and when you do, you have Feelings Of Missing Out (FOMO). You overextend your commitments, and later resent them.
2. You are a human "doing mobile." you know, constantly in motion, running on automatic and when you stop you feel out of place? The thought of taking a break will put you behind with your "to do" list, creating more anxiety and concerns for you.
3. You are exhausted, overworked, spent. You even know that you need to stop, yet you can't seem to get off the "doing mobile."

Take Time Out

Taking a moment for a brief time out can actually help you reboot and allow you to accomplish more in a shorter period than you imagine. I know you're probably wondering how that can happen when you're overwhelmed, but believe me, it's the truth!

Rebooting:

- Realigns your energy field.
- Helps you focus and gain clarity.
- Allows you to get out of your head and into your body.

If you are a skeptic, I invite you to experiment with the following. This is a simple formula to consider when you're overwhelmed and want to get off the "doing mobile."

- Stop what you are doing; this ceases the momentum.
- Take a deep breath, which brings you into your physical body.
- Go outside or someplace to get you out of the space you've been in.
- Distract yourself by doing something you enjoy.

Step 10
Mindfulness, Law of Attraction, Gratitude and Appreciation

You are an amazing creator and manifester! Everything you have in your life and have experienced has shown you just how incredibly powerful you are. Yes, even the not so pleasant experiences are part of your creative ability.

1. When you focus on the things you do not have, you create more of not having what you do not have. The same is true about focusing on things that you love. Your mind knows no difference between polarity and continues to create.
2. When you add gratitude and appreciation to the mix you create more situations to appreciate and be grateful and for. Having gratitude in the present moment—no matter how messy the moment is, allows you to receive more situations. It's an energy thing!
3. I define appreciation as gratitude on steroids. Even though the words *gratitude* and *appreciation* vibrate at a higher energetic frequency, appreciation is slightly higher.

More Gratitude and Appreciation

No matter what you have experienced in your life, there is always something to be grateful for and to appreciate.

- If life has got you feeling stuck, shift your focus to being grateful for the simple things you have, such as a roof over head, etc.
- Gratitude implies that you overcame something such as a challenge.
- Appreciation is the flow of allowing.
- When you show appreciation to those around you and appreciate what you have, you are magnetic to others who want to continue being around you and serve you.

There is always something to be grateful for and to appreciate. Both open doors for you to receive the blessings and abundance that life has to offer.

Step 11
Being vs. Doing

Do you ever feel as if you are "doing mobile?" You know, constantly in motion, running on automatic and when you stop you feel out of place? We are programmed by society that not being in constant motion is not okay. The sad truth is you may have become lopsided, out of balance, stressed, tired, and even sick as a result.

1. You as a human were never intended to be a machine, running on automatic, trying to make something happen, pushing a boulder up a hill. You have bought into the concept that you have to work hard to prove your worth.
2. There is nothing to figure out, yet you think you need to have a solution for everything. It's as if your ego needs to be in control of the project.
3. You have worked harder instead of smarter. You know the current state you're in is unsustainable, yet you carry on, not knowing how to stop and get off the "doing mobile."

Moving From Doing To Being

There is another way—a simpler more balanced way. You are skeptical and know your current way is not leading you to the more balanced life you crave.

- Being is about allowing, receiving, being in the flow, feeling, being heart-centered and fully present in your body in real-time.
- Doing is controlling, forcing, thinking, manipulating, analyzing, being in your head, living in the past and/or in the future.
- You need both *doing* and *being* to dance through life.
- When you start with *being,* then *doing* becomes divine.

Allow yourself just to *be.*

- Spend time with a mindful activity, be in nature, start a hobby or something that takes you out of your mind.
- Immerse your senses. Feel and get connected with the earth.
- Being in the present moment you connect more with your inner wisdom. You're receptive to the next divine thing to do.
- Then move into divine doing, accomplish that and then return to divine being.

Step 12
Self-Compassion

You are probably the hardest on yourself. You hold yourself to high standards that you don't impose on others. You are probably a perfectionist as well. Sound familiar?

1. You judge and criticize yourself, take things very seriously, and may even beat yourself up for not being better. This is an endless cycle.
2. How you feel about yourself contributes to your self-worth and self-confidence. When things aren't perfect or don't go as you expect, you're devastated and spiral down the rabbit hole.
3. Having compassion for yourself is an act of kindness. It is loving yourself enough to know you're doing the best you can. You are good enough, worthy enough, and valued no matter what you are currently experiencing.

More on Self-Compassion

Having self-compassion allows you to create peace of mind for yourself. I consider this a game changer. It has been part of my life as a recovering perfectionist. If you are an empath, intuitive, and highly sensitive person (HSP), you are good at having compassion for others, but sometimes ignore your own needs.

Did you know that self-compassion:

- Allows you to receive from yourself what you give to others and what you desire for yourself;
- Quiets your inner critic;
- Has no right, wrong, or perfect ways—just possibilities;
- Helps you cope better when life feels like it is falling apart;
- Allows you to accept your reality even when it is not ideal.

If compassion does not include yourself, it is incomplete.

- Be kind and understanding to yourself.
- You are a continuous work in progress.
- Allow yourself to live in the moment.

Step 13
Making Peace With Uncertainty and Fear

If you've learned anything in your life, it's that the only certain thing in life is uncertainty. With all the instability, fear, chaos, and drama in the world, it can be daunting just to step out your front door.

1. There is much more noise in our world today than ever before, thanks to instant access to news, social media, and topics that propagate fear and the unknown.
2. You may not know what to believe, and discerning truth can be a minefield as to what is real and what is fabricated.
3. You may feel as if you're going crazy, or going down the rabbit hole of no return. You may doubt and second-guess yourself, even though you feel in your gut that you're correct.

Taking Your Power Back

You do have a choice. You are in control of your life, even though you may see the illusion of it falling apart.

- You are a sovereign divine being who has free will. You have a right to make decisions on your terms, no matter what others are telling you.
- You always have a choice and can decide for yourself.
- Trust your gut feelings on hunches you're experiencing. If something feels off to you, honor your feelings.
- Remove yourself from uncomfortable experiences and situations; this is part of self-care.
- It is okay to question things; this is part of discernment.
- Turn off the news!
- Limit your time on social media!

Your choices may not be in alignment with what you hear from others, from the media, and other universal platforms. However, your choices are the right thing for you. Remember this:

> *I am safe, secure, and protected as I walk the earth as a sovereign being.*

Step 14
Listening and Trusting Your Inner Wisdom

Have you ever had a hunch to not do something, but you ignored it and did it anyway, only to later regret your decision? You are not alone. In fact, you probably talked yourself out of the correct choice for you the first time around.

1. Too often you second-guess yourself, even though you feel the right decision in your bones, gut, or heart. You can trust those feelings. They are impulses from your soul guiding you to make the right decision for you.
2. You're on the fence about making a decision, whether it's about your health, relationships, finances, or even work. You analyze and possibly overanalyze all the possibilities.
3. Your mind is racing with all the what ifs. Are you making the safe decision, or the one that your inner wisdom is guiding you to make?

Simple Steps to Trust Yourself

You may feel as if you're making an emotional decision if you follow your gut instincts. This is not true. You are listening to yourself.

- Give yourself permission to follow your hunches, gut feelings, and other somatic feelings without judging or criticizing them.
- Trust your feelings; they are your inner guidance system to help you make the correct decisions for you.
- You are a sovereign being, with free will and rights here on earth. Trust what you are receiving without second-guessing yourself; it may save your life.
- Be mindful where you give your power away in life. For example, do you let mandates from the government make decisions for you when your gut is screaming at you to not comply?
- Our inner wisdom is our saving grace, even though it may not align with what is occurring around us.
- It's okay to make decisions for yourself based on your inner guidance.

Step 15

Showing up in Your Life: Aligning Your Mind, Body, and Soul

Everywhere you go, there you are. How you show up in life is not compartmentalized into boxes. For example, how you are at work is how you are in life. Everything is interconnected as a matrix.

1. This is a game changer for you! You are the constant variable in all situations. Who you are creates your reality.
2. Once you are aware of this, there is no turning back, only moving forward. You are in charge. You are the captain of your ship.
3. Say what you mean and mean what you say. Your body, mind, and soul are constantly in dialog with each other. Are you part of the conversation, and are you listening?

This Is Where the Magic Happens!

I invite you to start putting yourself first on your list. Make yourself a priority in your life! Do what your heart is telling you! Listen to your heart intelligence; it has great wisdom.

- Release the emergency brake that is holding you back from moving forward in your life.
- Showing up in your life is at the end of your comfort zone. It's okay to be scared.
- Feel the fear and do it anyway.
- You are important enough to you to show up for yourself!
- Remember, you are loved, appreciated, valued and honored for who you are!
- The world and others need your gifts and talents!

Put yourself out there and take a chance. YOUR confidence will *soar* and will allow you to continue this path of magic!

When you commit and show up in your life, I guarantee that serendipity, magic, and alchemy will be yours!

You've finished. Before you go…

Tweet/Post/Share that you finished this book.

Please star rate this book.

Reviews are solid gold to writers. Please take a few minutes to give us some itty bitty feedback.

ABOUT THE AUTHOR

Dr. Dolores Fazzino DNP is a nurse practitioner, medical intuitive, and an energy whisperer. With over 40 years in the healthcare industry, she has assisted in over 18,500 surgical procedures and has helped people heal in ways they never thought possible. She is a pioneer and visionary practitioner who uses energy healing to create true health and lasting wellness.

Gifted since childhood with intuitive abilities, she is an empathic highly sensitive person (HSP), she is a medical intuitive, healer, and visionary who has always been on the cutting edge. She worked under the revolutionary Dr. Bernie Siegel, an international expert and surgeon in the field of cancer treatment and complementary holistic medicine in the 1980s.

As a young adult, Dolores witnessed the miraculous and spontaneous healing of her father's health condition, using alternative modalities. After that, she changed her area of study from music to healthcare and has devoted her career to offering other possibilities for healing in addition to traditional western medicine.

Dr. Fazzino believes healing is a multi-faceted and interconnected process. Our current health-care system is exceptional at addressing the physical needs of individuals. However, the mental, emotional, and spiritual needs are lacking in our current healthcare system. When those needs are also addressed, healing, lasting health, and true wellness are achieved.

Recognizing the many gaps in healthcare, Dr. Fazzino takes us beyond the mind-body paradigm to include spirituality in wellness. Through her companies, **Recovering Healthcare,** and **Spiritual Wellness for Life,** this distinguished wellness practitioner offers customized programs and strategies to prepare clients by combining traditional medicine, energy healing, and intuitive counseling to assist clients in moving through dis-*ease,* life challenges, and reconnecting to their inner self with grace and ease

She earned a doctor of nursing practice (DNP) degree in 2008 from Case Western Reserve University, one of the top nursing programs in the nation. With her education and expertise, Dr. Fazzino has developed an innovative program to support patients and their loved ones before, during, and after surgery.

As founder of **Concierge Surgical Coaching®**, she is the industry leader in preparing patients to heal faster and more completely from surgery, chronic illness, and other health and wellness concerns.

Additionally, she has authored several books including Amazon international best sellers, *"The Wellness Universe Complete Guide to Self-Care: 25 Tools to Stress Relief,"* and, *"The Wellness*

Universe Complete Guide to Self-Care: 25 Tool for Happiness." Her other books include, *"54 Tips to Maneuver Through the Healthcare System,"* and, *"Spiritual Wellness for Life."*

Dr. Fazzino is a speaker who presents her vast knowledge of topics related to healthcare and mind-body wellness internationally. She has presented at the Wellness Universe SoulTreat Retreats, Omega Institute, Association of Perioperative Nurses (AORN), National Nurses in Business Associates (NNBA), California Dialysis Council, and Palomar Pomerado Healthcare.

If you enjoyed this Itty Bitty® Book you may also like …

- **Your Amazing Itty Bitty® Aging Well Book** – Michele McHenry
- **Your Amazing Itty Bitty® Stress Reduction Book** – Denise Thomson
- **Your Amazing Itty Bitty® Heal Your Body Book** – Patricia Garza Pinto

Or any of the many other Itty Bitty® books available online at www.ittybittypublishing.com

Made in the USA
Coppell, TX
19 January 2023